RUBANK EDUCATIONAL LIBRARY No. 63

Soloist Folio

FOR
E♭ ALTO SAXOPHONE
with Piano Accompaniment

CONTENTS

RUBANK®

HAL•LEONARD®
CORPORATION
7777 W. BLUEMOUND RD. P.O. BOX 13819 MILWAUKEE, WI 53213

Hymn to the Sun

Transcription for E♭ Saxophone

Piano

N. RIMSKY–KORSAKOW
Transcribed by Carleton Colby

Copyright MCMXXXVIII by Rubank Inc., Chicago, Ill.
International Copyright Secured

Hungarian Dance No. 5

Piano

JOH. BRAHMS
Arr. by Henry W. Davis

Allegro

Copyright MCMXXXVIII by Rubank Inc.,Chicago,Ill.
International Copyright Secured

Flight of the Bumblebee

SCHERZO

Piano

N. RIMSKY-KORSAKOW

Cl.-Sax.-Xyl. & Mar.

Badine
Scherzo

Piano Acc.

GABRIEL—MARIE
Arr. by Henry W. Davis

Copyright MCMXXXVIII by Rubank Inc., Chicago, Ill.
International Copyright Secured

Le Secret

INTERMEZZO

PIANO

LEONARD GAUTIER
Arr. by Henry W. Davis

1st time to next strain
2nd time to Trio
Last time to Coda

Coppelia
Valse Lente

Piano

LEO DELIBES
Arr. by Henry W. Davis

Nimble Fingers

R.H. "DUKE" REHL

Copyright MCMXXVIII by Rubank Inc., Chicago, Ill.
International Copyright Secured

RUBANK Educational Library No. 63

Soloist Folio

FOR
Eb ALTO SAXOPHONE
with Piano Accompaniment

CONTENTS

RUBANK®

HAL•LEONARD® CORPORATION

7777 W. BLUEMOUND RD. P.O. BOX 13819 MILWAUKEE, WI 53213

Hymn to the Sun
Transcription for E♭ Saxophone

E♭ Alto Saxophone

N. RIMSKY-KORSAKOW
Transcribed by Carleton Colby

Copyright MCMXXXVIII by Rubank Inc., Chicago, Ill.
International Copyright Secured

Hungarian Dance No. 5

Eb Alto Saxophone

JOH. BRAHMS
Arr. by Henry W. Davis

Copyright MCMXXXVIII by Rubank Inc., Chicago, Ill.
International Copyright Secured

Flight of the [4] Bumblebee

SCHERZO

E♭ Alto Saxophone

N. RIMSKY KORSAKOW
Transcribed by H.W. Davis

6
Badine
Scherzo

Eb Alto Saxophone

GABRIEL–MARIE
Arr. by Henry W. Davis

Le Secret

INTERMEZZO

E♭ ALTO SAXOPHONE

LEONARD GAUTIER
Arr by Henry W. Davis

TRIO

Coppelia

10

Valse Lente

Eb Alto Saxophone

LEO DELIBES
Arr. by Henry W. Davis

Copyright MCMXXXVIII by Rubank Inc., Chicago, Ill.
International Copyright Secured

Nimble Fingers

Eb ALTO SAXOPHONE

R. H. "DUKE" REHL

Andante Sostenuto

Nimble Fingers

SAXOPEAL

E♭ ALTO SAXOPHONE

NEAL. B DUNN

Saxopeal

16
Tiptoes

Eb Alto Saxophone

WILSON JOHN FISHER

Copyright MCMXXXVII by Rubank Inc., Chicago, Ill.
International Copyright Secured

17
E♭ Alto Saxophone

Piano

Solo

mf

Piano

Solo

rit.

mf a tempo

f a tempo

1

rit.

2

cresc.

f

Tiptoes

Carnival of Venice

Air Varie

Alto Saxophone -

HENRY W. DAVIS

Alto Saxophone

NARCISSUS

1st Alto Saxophone (Solo)

ETHELBERT NEVIN
Arr. by Herman A. Hummel

Nimble Fingers

Nimble Fingers

Nimble Fingers

Nimble Fingers

Nimble Fingers

SAXOPEAL

PIANO

NEAL B. DUNN

Saxopeal

rall. - poco - a - poco

Saxopeal

Piano

Saxopeal

CODA

Con brio

Tiptoes

Piano

WILSON JOHN FISHER

Copyright MCMXXXVII by Rubank Inc., Chicago, Ill.
International Copyright Secured

Tiptoes

Tiptoes

Tiptoes

Carnival of Venice

Air Varie

Piano

HENRY W. DAVIS

Copyright MCMXLII by Rubank, Inc., Chicago, Ill.
International Copyright Secured

Piano

Elegante

Piano

NARCISSUS

ETHELBERT NEVIN
Arr. by Herman A. Hummel